THE WORK OF THE USHER

ALVIN D. JOHNSON

THE
WORK
OF THE
USHER

JUDSON PRESS®
VALLEY FORGE

THE WORK OF THE USHER

Copyright © 1966
Judson Press
Valley Forge, PA 19482-0851

Sixteenth Printing, 1988

International Standard Book No. 0-8170-0356-8
Library of Congress Catalog Card No. 66 – 22519

The name JUDSON PRESS is registered as a trademark in the United States Patent Office.

Printed in the United States of America

CONTENTS

84200

Other books of interest:

The Deacon at Work
Frederick A. Agar

The Deacon in a Changing Church
Donald F. Thomas

The Work of the Church Treasurer
Thomas E. McLeod

The Work of the Church Trustee
Orlando L. Tibbetts

The Work of the Clerk
Zelotes Grenell and Agnes Goss

The Work of the Deacon and Deaconess
Harold Nichols

Work of the Pastoral Relations Committee
Emmett V. Johnson

PREFACE

THE ADVICE TO PUT ONE'S BEST FOOT FORWARD ought to be as applicable to churches as to individuals, particularly inasmuch as the church has so much to offer to so many people. The usher is in that strategic position where worshipers obtain first impressions, and therefore his role is highly significant. This book attempts to point out what the usher's ideals and attitudes should be, and it offers suggestions and challenges to him as he sees himself as a teamworker in a large complex. This material is offered with the knowledge that generalizations cannot apply to every church, for each church presents problems which grow out of its own uniqueness. In spite of this implied need for adaptations, the author hopes that something will be contained herein that will help every church usher to make his church a better one.

In order to enhance the value of this book, a special checklist for the usher is added, as well as suggestions for growth in his work. There are also sample letters and diagrams of the work of the usher. These devices are incorporated to help the usher to be at his best at all times.

The author is indebted to unnumbered experienced ushers whose capabilities have reached these pages in one way or another. To some of these who may read this book he expresses the hope that they may discover some new technique or be heartened in their continuing service. The book is offered with the prayer that God may bless the ministry and effectiveness of every usher as he seeks joyfully to be "a doorkeeper in the house of the Lord."

ALVIN D. JOHNSON

New Haven
July 15, 1966

1. THE ROLE OF THE USHER

THE HOST OR HOSTESS IN THE RESTAURANT is the efficient and gracious person who knows where there is a readied table, of sufficient size for the number of guests in the party, with an available waiter. The usher at the concert glances at a pair of tickets and quickly leads the purchasers down the aisle to the exact location. The elevator starter in the lobby of a tall office building tells the visitor not only the desired floor, but also whether to turn to the right or the left when he gets out of the elevator. Railroad conductors, guards in sports stadiums, building hostesses, airplane stewardesses, even librarians all are charged with getting people to the proper location at the right time. Each serves as a bridge from one phase of experience to another. The church usher is a part of such a tradition as he leads individuals into the atmosphere of the church service.

When visiting a synagogue, the author was met at the door by a gentleman who had the unique gift of making him feel welcome and at ease on his first visit. Though the Jewish house of worship was strangely different from that of his own experience and religious heritage, he found it beautiful, appealing, and worshipful. Although he was in the midst of a community of people who were somehow different, there was something in the usher's manner which seemed to convey the knowledge that he was wanted here. This usher had represented the synagogue and its people at their best.

Similarly, it may be seen that the church usher occupies a strategic office in the life and image of the church. He is first a person to be respected and appreciated. He is the embodiment of the gracious spirit of the religious group. And he is more than this: Often unknowingly, he is the friend who shares in making the lonely feel cared for, the bereaved see hope, the sinner feel forgiveness, the discouraged feel cheered, the rich feel generous, the poor feel rich, and everyone feel enjoined to unselfish love for his neighbor. In short, he is the instrument who introduces the individual to every practical expression of the church's mission, and to the presence of the Almighty.

2. THE PERSON WHO USHERS

AFTER THE ENTERING INDIVIDUAL has been confronted by the facade of the church building, he next comes face to face with a person. This person is serving in the role of an usher, but he meets the guest as one person to another. Whether man or woman, mature or youthful, he is, in fact, more a person than a professional usher. What is there in this usher's personality and training that enables him quickly to captivate the one who is entering and lead him, spiritually as well as physically, into the beauty of the sanctuary?

No person is born an usher. He becomes an efficient, practicing usher only by means of training and experience. Ushering can be taught and learned. That meaning which underlies the task must be the springboard for the accomplishment of a proficiency which at first glance looks easy, but in reality is elu-

sive. Every well-seasoned usher knows this fact, and
for this reason none of the observations and suggestions in the following pages will appear to him as
prosaic or painfully obvious. The veteran will continue to refresh his skills and the novice will en-
deavor to make himself as effective as possible.

A PERSON OF PRAYER

The foundation of the usher's preparation, as in
any Christian service, is prayer. The work begins,
continues, and accomplishes its ultimate purposes in
prayer. The author recalls a kind and much-beloved
deacon who never failed to call briefly and silently
upon the Father to bless each person as he extended
his hand in a welcome. No person thus greeted can
escape the warmth and sincerity of such a meeting.
The hearty handshake of a politician seeking another
vote should not be mistaken for anything more than
what it is intended to be. The kiss of the actress
while she is on stage, and her pseudo-endearing term
"Darling" are not evidences of truth, but are to be
recognized as merely the shallow niceties that they
are. But, on the other hand, an usher who has pray-
erfully thought through the solemn privileges and
opportunities of his task will be recognized as a sin-
cere guide and friend.

A PERSON WHO THINKS

The prospective usher's mental preparation is almost equally important. He is willing not only to think but to spend some time in practice before he begins to carry out his duties. Perhaps he will visit several other churches of varying sizes and floor plans, to observe their special problems of ushering, and how each one reaches or fails to reach a happy solution. His philosophy, like the Apostle Paul's, is that he has not yet attained, but is always attaining.

In his own church the usher is ever on the alert to spot any signs of awkwardness and to discover better ways of performing his functions. He wants to maintain a living and intelligent approach toward certain desired results, and thereby he guards against thoughtless repetitions of movements which are lacking in dignity or good taste. One of the greatest temptations of any regular position is that of getting into a rut, but the dedicated usher will seek to be creative in his work. In fact, in everything he plans and carries out, he aspires that his work may be a glad and worthy service to the Lord.

The usher's voice should be well modulated, and used in such a way that he sounds respectful. Regardless of the usher's feelings, his voice should never

give the impression that he is bored, anxious, chid-
ing, patronizing, obsequious, boisterous, or flippant.
Every word should be uttered with the utmost po-
liteness and tact.

One desirable attribute of an usher, frequently apt
to be overlooked, is keen hearing. If it is necessary
for him to hear any words spoken by the guest, he
should hear the first time, and not find it necessary
to ask that the words be either repeated or shouted.
This does not imply that the usher may not use a
hearing aid if necessary. With or without an aid,
he should be able to hear.

A lively sense of stewardship is essential in the
person who foresees the opportunity of being an
usher. This means that he will exercise a rigid responsibility in all of his relationships with the church
and his fellow ushers. He is a giver, rather than a re-
ceiver. He has an understanding of not only the hu-
man factor in the act of worship but also the signifi-
cance of the presence of God, and he knows that he
stands as the representative of that higher reality.

This attitude of stewardship will express itself in
a number of specific ways, centering upon the idea
that the usher is dependable. He is a part of a group
of ushers, a part of the church at worship, and a part
of the kingdom of God. Regularity and promptness

are virtues which should be cultivated. He should be where he has said he will be, and should be there on time. He should be considerate of the worshipers and the other ushers, sensing their feelings, aiding in the cultivation of a group sense, and minimizing his own convenience. He will even take upon himself some discomfort in order to aid in providing a comfortable and reverent environment for the worshipers.

The usher's personal appearance should reflect his unseen attributes, which have been outlined. Suit, tie, shoes, and shirt, although they may vary with the local customs and the season, should be neat and conservative. Good grooming, with special attention to the nails, teeth, and hair, is imperative. It hardly seems necessary to warn that precautions should be taken against unpleasant odors from breath or body, and certainly that there should be no gum chewing while on duty. The ushers might well have certain aids at their disposal, such as a mirror and a shoe-shine kit. One good test of the propriety of personal appearance is the inability of anyone to remember what the usher was wearing.

The habits and traditions of the local situation must be considered in regard to certain devices which are sometimes used to identify the ushers, such as carnations, name plates, and badges. In some churches, these would be considered as helpful and acceptable while in others they would be thought of as ostentatious or affected. The pastor may have some thoughts on this matter, as well as ideas he would like to have carried out, and of course his wishes should be seriously considered.

In personality, demeanor, cleanliness, and appearance, the usher gives every evidence of being a gentleman who is cultured and sensitive to the needs of others.

3. ORGANIZING FOR ACTION

IN OUR DEMOCRATIC SOCIETY groups of people seem to do their most efficient work when they are organized. When the individuals meet with one another from time to time, agree to some general rules of conduct, and accept specific assignments, they come to an understanding of the total task and how it may be accomplished. Without such an understanding there is autocracy, anarchy, or lethargy. Among a group of ushers autocracy would prevail if one individual who pretended to possess all the necessary knowledge handed out to each usher specific directives to be followed obediently and unquestioningly. The opposite of this would be anarchy, in which each usher would presumably do his best to accomplish whatever he saw that needed attention. Such a haphazard system would often find two or more ushers bent upon doing the same thing while some other

function was left unthought-of and undone. Either
extreme, autocracy or anarchy, can lead to a lack
of interest in the work of ushering, if lethargy has not
crept into the membership in some other fashion.

EXTENT OF ORGANIZATION

The organization of the ushers should be no more
than necessary — just enough — to accomplish the
functions for which ushers exist. It should be re-
membered that the entire church is the focal point
of the Christian fellowship, and no one of its affili-
ated activities should achieve such emphasis as to
command loyalties of its members which rightfully
belong to the parent body. Too often a board, a society, or a fellowship group becomes so highly organized that its members lose sight of its real reason
for existence. The ushers are not the fathers of the
church: the church is the father of the ushers. Therefore, an ushers' organization is to be carried on for
the express purpose of making the church effective
in its peculiar mission. This does not prevent the
observance of such social functions as make for good
fellowship, so long as the principal purpose of the
ushers' organization is kept in mind.

In view of the need for some degree of organization, it would be advisable to hold meetings as fre-

quently as necessary. For the proper conduct of a meeting there should be a chairman, and in a large church a vice-chairman may be desired. For the keeping of records there should be a secretary (or a secretary-treasurer, if the group maintains funds for any purpose). The general rule regarding the extent of organization should be that there be only enough of it to accomplish the ushering functions, and the less the better.

At each function when ushers are needed, there should be a head usher, whose duty it will be to supervise the movements of the ushers. This head usher may be the same individual for a term of office, or each usher may be designated to take a turn as head usher for a single church service. If desired, the chairman himself may be chosen to be the head usher. The important need is that there surely be a head usher on hand on every occasion.

MEETINGS

Three aims should be kept in view as the reasons for holding meetings of the ushers. First, many minds are better than one, and the sharing of ideas is important and productive. Second, the ushers themselves should devise and set forth the specific plans and procedures of their work, always under the advice and guidance of the pastor. Third, a desirable team spirit is fostered as individuals learn to know each other better and feel more at ease in each other's presence.

Continued learning leads to success. The most successful business men are those who do not grow tired of study and planning. It is so in the work of the church. Ushers are more proficient if they continue to learn. Therefore, the meeting of ushers should sometimes be organized into a learning experience. The value of this practice can be seen when it is realized that among the ushers there may be the new faces of those who never were ushers before. Therefore, perhaps once a year, it would be profitable to review this manual and reevaluate the work as it is being done. Not only will this refresh the memory, but some detail might be the stimulus for new ideas not brought forth in the manual, which would enhance the smooth functioning of the ushering.

A concert orchestra, even if it has been building a reputation for many years, reviews its performance constantly. Each composition is rehearsed laboriously and minutely, so that its performance does not seem stale and listless. Is a concert more important than proficient leadership in the church? This re-

hearsal technique can be used to advantage in the
ushers' meeting. Various situations which call for the
cooperation, knowledge, and tact of the ushers can
be rehearsed or role-played. Why not go into the
church sanctuary and practice the offering procedure? Other procedures may also be tried and
polished when the congregation is not present.

The meeting is an opportune time for working out
special problems. The ushers of one church had
drifted into a habit which was disturbing to some
of the worshipers during the offering. When one
usher had finished taking the offering in the aisle
assigned to him, he would then help another usher
by beginning at the back row and working forward
until he met his fellow usher midway down the aisle.
At every row the worshiper at the end of the pew
was startled and astonished as the well-meaning
usher appeared silently and suddenly from over his
shoulder. When this practice was drawn to the attention of the ushers, they devised a plan whereby
the assisting usher began his work at a previously-
marked pew and, like the other ushers, proceeded,
pew by pew, toward the rear. Other similar problems are worthy of discussion, such as that of the
rear-pew squatter and how to encourage him to se-
lect a position in a more forward location.

ASSIGNMENTS

Ushers may be secured by vote of the congregation, by appointment, and by the personal solicitation of the pastor, head usher, or chairman of the ushers. Sometimes a recruitment letter may be sent to prospective ushers (see Appendix), although it has been found that letters fail to elicit the response which can often be more readily gained by personal contact.

An assignment schedule should be drawn up well in advance. This may take into consideration not only the ushers who are to be on duty on specific dates, but in more thoroughly planned situations what are the duties of each usher on that date. The schedule may be planned for at least three months in advance, and possibly for a full year. In the latter case, allowances must be made for unforeseen circumstances. A sample assignment chart may be found in the Appendix on page 58.

Each usher should understand where he fits into the whole pattern of ushering. Assuming that not every usher is needed for every church service, a master plan should show exactly who are to usher on any given occasion. Further, the specific duties of each usher on that occasion should be designated.

A sure method of informing each usher of his precise responsibility is the assignment letter (see Appendix).

DEPLOYMENT

If left to themselves, individuals who are supposed to usher are tempted to gather in a sociable little group in one spot, unaware of the clock and the assembling worshipers. In order to insure prompt, helpful service to those who have come to church, there should be a plan, and the head usher should see that the plan is in operation. Every usher should know his location and his duties in that location. This information may be given to him by letter or telephone at some time before the day of the church service, or upon his arrival (presuming that all ushers naturally report for duty about twenty minutes before the beginning of the service). Notwithstanding, every usher is alive to the needs in all parts of the sanctuary, and is always prepared to lend his assistance.

A small bulletin board at the head usher's station might have a diagram of the seating arrangement of the sanctuary (see example, p. 24). On it the station and the area of responsibility for each usher should be shown. This diagram can be duplicated so that a

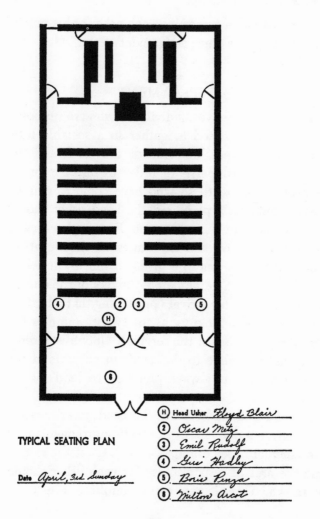

TYPICAL SEATING PLAN

Date *April, 3rd Sunday*

(H) Head Usher *Floyd Blair*
(2) *Oscar Metz*
(3) *Emil Rudolf*
(4) *Gus Hadley*
(5) *Boris Pinza*
(6) *Milton Arcot*

24

new copy may be posted for each church service, or, if advantageous, a copy handed to each usher. Either use of the diagram will be a brief but efficient way of acquainting each usher with his station and area of service for the day.

KEEPING RECORDS

The records kept by ushers are usually simple, albeit significant. Under the date and time of the service it is important to know the condition of the weather and the number of people in attendance. Occasionally, for a special study, it becomes desirable to ascertain also the number of a particular group who are present, such as children under 12, men, or how many sit in the balcony. The number present is acutely related to the date. Christmas, Easter, and anniversaries, for instance, are usually seasons of the greatest attendance. The location of the church also has a marked bearing upon attendance. If the church is in a typical town or city within two hundred miles of a popular resort area, the attendance may be expected to diminish during the resort's big season. However, if the church is in the resort itself, the attendance will be greatest during the vacation season. As for the weather, it is to be expected that rain, fog, or snow will tempt people to

stay at home, whereas a particularly beautiful week-
end may lure them out into the country, or into another state to pay a long-planned visit to Aunt Patti
and Cousin Frank.

The attendance and weather record will be re-
corded by the head usher in a book retained for the
purpose. A page which has several columns is useful
for displaying the records for more than one year, so
that comparisons may be made. The number of people present may be ascertained by having each usher
count the people in his area as he receives the offering. The head usher then performs a simple addition
to obtain the total. Also, the head usher may go to
some strategic but inconspicuous place where he
may try to count all of the people, thus verifying the
results obtained by the other ushers.

4. THE CHURCH SERVICE

THE USHER IS A THOROUGHLY TRAINED LEADER in the house of the Lord. As the members of the congregation arrive, he is the first person they meet. Because first impressions are important, it follows that in meeting, greeting, and leading a person into the church he bears almost awesome responsibility. He escorts people into the meeting house of God. In doing so, he becomes the bridge which leads to the greatest possible contrast of environment — from the concerns of the secular world, sometimes humdrum and sometimes busy and exciting or fearful and perplexing, to the place where in quietness and meditation man seeks spiritual renewal.

SEATING

Whether one is being seated in a sports stadium, an opera house, an outdoor Easter sunrise service, or in the church sanctuary, the basic problems of seating are similar. Many individuals arriving at the same time need guidance to avoid hindering or retarding the free movement of each one. The specific purpose for which each one has come to the church demands that he be able to see, hear, be comfortable, enjoy, and participate in the worship experience. The usher is a strategist who, in spite of changing conditions and disconcerting surprises, promotes the free and apparently unhurried flow of people.

As the worshiper enters the church's main door, he has already noticed whether the property has been cared for as befits the house of the Lord. He is favorably impressed if the outside bulletin board is clean and has no rusty letters, the lawn is well trimmed, and the door opens easily without squeaking. "Somebody seems to care," he observes to himself. At this moment someone approaches him with an outstretched hand and a smile which reveals genuine pleasure. Yes, someone does care. He has just been greeted by an usher who is demonstrating that this entire church cares.

The greeting given by this usher is neither casual nor artificial. He was stationed just inside the door (or, in some cases, outside the door) for the express purpose of being the first one to greet every person. Visitors and strangers are especially impressed by this touch of warm friendliness. Over a foundation of personal prayer this usher is a symbol of that which his church represents: Christianity in all of its appeal, understanding, love, and hope; the atmosphere of worship which brings respite from the world; peace and joy, and the sense of mission which leads one back into the world for Christian witness.

The worshiper now advances into the sanctuary where he can see the entire place of worship. He notes that even though the back row is rather well occupied, people are in every part of the room. Some are already seated and others are just getting settled. Another usher is pleasantly gaining the attention of the worshiper. He leads the way to a pew which seems to be somewhat centrally located and then hands the worshiper a copy of the church bulletin. The worshiper notes that, although there are two others in the same pew, no one was entrenched next to the aisle to be climbed over and trampled upon. He wonders how the ushers have accomplished such a feat which makes things so convenient.

The worshiper now sits back with gratification that he has gained two new friends in the two ushers who have led him to this spot with such real sincerity. He notes that there are about as many people in front of him as behind him, and that he has been seated in the location which he himself would have chosen, had he been able to see it when he first entered. How did the wise usher know how to do this? The worshiper reflects for a moment upon what had happened.

The second usher had actually asked him where he preferred to be seated, but so imperceptibly that the worshiper hardly realized it. Then the usher had quietly indicated that he was to be followed, and before long he was standing before the well-chosen pew. An understanding mind is important in an usher. He must comprehend every situation quickly. When someone enters on crutches, or wearing a hearing aid, or accompanied by children, he knows where this person will gain the most benefit from the church service. When a handicapped one, a young woman advanced in pregnancy, or an elderly person in need of assistance comes in, he instinctively knows where this individual would like best to be seated.

Care and forethought had indeed been given by the ushers in this church. Church bulletins were not handed to worshipers until they were entering the pews, minimizing the hazards of drawing attention away from walking. By agreement with the pastor, no one was seated during Scripture reading, prayer, or special music.

On an occasion when it is known that there will be a small congregation in a large sanctuary, some sections of the room should not be used. These should be indicated by decorative cords placed on the pews before any worshipers arrive. In any case, ushers should become adept at seating the people in such a way that large areas of empty pews are not evident, for these are disconcerting to the pastor, choir, and congregation. If the sanctuary has a center aisle, the atmosphere of worship will be aided by avoiding its use after the service has begun. This practice alleviates embarrassment to the latecomer and disturbance to the worshipers.

Every one who enters is to be respected by the usher as a child of God. The person who is humbly dressed should be treated with the same consideration and dignity as the one who obviously is expensively dressed. The usher is there to help the young, the old, the rich, the poor — everyone.

MANNER AND DEPORTMENT

There once was a little boy who, not having heard his parents accurately, thought that ushers were "shushers." Probably he had often needed "shushing." Of course, the usher should be on hand and ready to deal with any eventuality including noisy children, but the ideal usher is quite inconspicuous. He accomplishes his duties wholly without ostentation or flourish. He is on hand when he is needed, but at other times his presence is not obvious.

For the usher, a friendly but not too familiar manner is important. His must be a subdued friendliness. To be jovial, too jolly, or loud in the Lord's house is not fitting. The guest can be made to feel at home by a smile, a direct glance into his eyes, and perhaps a warm handclasp. A quiet, well-modulated tone of voice can carry as much warmth and welcome as the booming greeting which might be fitting at the lodge meeting or in the firehouse. The usher who can anticipate the needs of the guest and then quietly go about meeting these needs is the most helpful.

The usher remembers that he is one of a team, and not a lone star. He works in close cooperation with the others. His aim, like the aim of the whole team, is that of making each individual in the congregation feel welcome, comfortable, and ready for worship.

Like the rest of the congregation, ushers are worshipers. They do not converse with one another, laugh, or even show the slightest inclination to be inattentive to the service. In short, they should never be the source of disturbance or distraction. Instead, they should be leaders in worship, engaging in the worship experience, rising when the congregation should rise, sitting when they should sit, and praying during the time of prayer.

TENDING THE CONGREGATION

Whenever many people are gathered in one place, the unexpected can be expected to happen. To be sure, most of the emergencies will be of a minor nature, but the usher must be conditioned to respond to any crisis, even a disaster. His position is such that the people will look to him for leadership in such occurrences as fire, a bomb scare, a riot or other civil disturbance, sudden death, or the severe illness of someone present. Therefore he needs to have thought out well in advance what he would do in a crisis, so that he can respond with calm, capable leadership if the need should arise. He should know how to make use of all emergency exits, where to secure first aid, and how to call the fire department, the police, or medical help. He should recognize that, even though he may have seated himself in the congregation at a certain point in the service, he is

still responsible for returning to his post and giving
any kind of emergency assistance or direction which
is needed and is within his power.

There may, of course, be some lesser emergencies
and discomforts during any church hour. The room
grows too stuffy or too hot or too cold. The children
in another room become noisy. Someone has a
coughing spell. A baby starts to cry, and another
child begs his daddy for some candy which daddy
has forgotten to bring.

Is the idea of tending the congregation reminiscent
of a shepherd and his flock? There could be many
less apt similes, for it is nearly so. The usher should
actually tend his congregation as though they were
his flock of sheep. He is constantly aware of needs,
and is constantly prepared to alleviate many such
unexpected situations as coughs, sudden illness, or
a bleeding nose. If there is a doctor in the congregation, the usher knows where he is seated, and if
there is none present he knows how to summon one
promptly. Items which may well be kept at the head
usher's station are such aids as smelling salts, a
pitcher of water, paper cups, and cough drops. Not
only does such preparation demonstrate a concern
for those who suddenly find themselves in distress,
but it protects the meditations of others.

Every physical facility and service provided by the church is a part of the usher's resources for tending the congregation. Among such advantages are the nursery and kindergarten departments and their supervisors and other helpers. All rest rooms should not only be marked, but the usher should be able to give concise directions to reach them. An alert usher will immediately recognize that the guest who wears a hearing aid may wish to be seated in a pew which is equipped with an earphone.

THE OFFERING

Almost every church service includes an offering, occasionally called a collection. Actually, the offering is more than a mere collection. It is a symbol of the sacrifice of all of life which is made by the Christian. *Offering* refers to life and substance; *collection* reminds one of a tax. The offering is a love gift to God and a symbol of the deeper consecration and dedication of the worshiper. It should be a high and solemn time in the worship.

Although there are various orders for the offering, the procedures of the ushers are similar in most cases. A prayer may either precede or follow the reception of the offering. If the prayer comes before the offering, there is often a musical response or the

Doxology later when the ushers present the offering. The ushers who participate in receiving the offering should each be assigned to a definite area. Upon some inconspicuous signal, they proceed down the aisle or aisles to the front of the sanctuary. In one church the signal is given by the minister's pressing a button beneath the lectern which, in turn, operates small red lights at the rear of the sanctuary. These lights are visible to the ushers, but are usually unnoticed by the rest of the worshipers. Care should be taken in the ushers' approach to the waiting minister, that the march forward be neither military nor rapid, nor should it in any way call attention to itself.

If the offering plates are kept at the front, a preappointed usher should distribute them to the other ushers. As soon as the prayer or other ceremony before the offering is concluded, the ushers proceed to their respective areas to receive the offering. When all ushers have completed this function, all march forward with the filled offering plates and stand quietly during the further dedicatory acts of the minister and people. Before or after this final dedication, according to the custom of the local church, the minister or one usher takes the plates from the ushers and deposits them in a prearranged place. The ushers then walk together to the rear of the sanctuary, where they first stood at the beginning of the offering. No usher takes a shortcut to any other point in the sanctuary. Whenever the architecture of the church and the arrangement of pews allow, it is especially pleasing to see the ushers move along the aisles in unison, so that they begin, continue, and end their work together.

The diagram of the seating arrangement of the sanctuary (page 24) is a helpful way of denoting the area for which each usher is responsible. If this diagram is posted where the ushers can study it, it will be a helpful reminder of the procedure for receiving the offering and a source of quick help for a new or substitute usher.

VARIATIONS

Each sanctuary and worship fellowship is different from all others. Therefore it is expedient that the ushers adapt all of their movements to the local situation, whatever it may be. The aim is to keep a normal, quiet flow to the worship service. Unfailingly, there will be latecomers. The usher knows both when and where to seat such people so that they will cause the least disturbance. He knows how to maintain quiet in the narthex or vestibule.

Not everyone who enters desires the personal attention of an usher, and care must be taken not to embarrass such people by forcing them to receive the usher's well-intentioned courtesies. Regular worshipers who are as dependable as "Old Faithful" may require no more than a quiet greeting and a bulletin. Each person who comes to worship should be treated as the individual that he is. After all, if there is any rule that *cannot* be broken, it is that any rule *should* be broken in order to avoid anything which would mar the worship of God.

5. BEFORE AND AFTER THE SERVICE

THE MINISTER HAS SPENT SEVERAL HOURS during the week in preparation for the church service. So has the sexton, and, in some churches during the winter, he has had to spend the entire preceding night in the building. Like many others who are briefly seen in action, both the pastor and the sexton have probably found it necessary to give unseen overtime in the performance of many details connected with their main responsibilities. The usher does not escape a similar responsibility, for there are many things to be done before and after the service.

READINESS OF THE SANCTUARY

Long before the earliest worshiper has arrived, the ushers should make sure that nothing has been left undone to provide a room which is ready in all respects for the people. It may be argued that this is the duty of the paid sexton, but it is often true that the sexton has more than he can do. A spirit of kind cooperation with the sexton is one of the privileges enjoyed by the usher.

It has been said that cleanliness is next to godliness. In the church, most worshipers are convinced that this is so. There may be any number of irritating oversights in the matter of cleanliness, such as dust on the narthex table or on one or two of the pews, or a tablecloth which has been brushed askew. Let the ushers be on hand to set such mishaps right.

Neatness is almost as important as cleanliness. Of all the spots where there is apt to be slovenliness, the pew racks take first place. These prominent items virtually seem to shout "Nobody cares!" or "Somebody cares!" All articles that belong in the pew racks, such as hymnbooks, Bibles, attendance cards, and pencils, should be arranged tidily and uniformly, so that each rack resembles every other. Dog-eared cards should be removed and all pencils sharpened. A jumbled clutter of last week's leftover bulletins and forgotten handkerchiefs amid hymnbooks sitting in all kinds of random positions reveals slipshod and careless ushering. The ushers should make sure that, whether it be the pew racks or any other part of the sanctuary's appurtenances, the entire appearance of the room silently says to the worshiper that he is both expected and welcome.

The lighting of the sanctuary requires constant vigilance on the part of the usher, particularly the head usher. Variations in architecture predetermine that some buildings will be dark and others very bright. If the sanctuary requires artificial light, an usher should decide how much light is needed and adjust the amount of light according to changing conditions of the clouds during the service. If the sanctuary is abundantly supplied with natural light, it often happens that the sun eventually reaches the faces of some of the worshipers, causing difficulty of vision if not actual discomfort, and this undue brilliance must immediately be corrected if possible. In no case should frantic motions or an outright announcement from the pulpit become necessary. The worshiper should have sufficient light, but not an excess of it, to read the hymnbook and Bible.

The quality of air in a room is more important than many people suppose it to be, and is easily overlooked. In the winter, air should be warm and flowing; in the summer, it should be the same, but then we call it "cool" and flowing. Moreover, a statistical figure called the temperature-humidity index is coming more and more into use in the summer. When this index of combined levels of temperature and relative humidity reaches 75, about half of the people are uncomfortable. In colonial days, when sermons were long and air was stale, ushers kept drowsy members of the congregation awake by tickling them with a squirrel's tail affixed to a long pole. In our own day, when methods are less drastic, we know that temperature and ventilation must be closely watched. Windows may need to be opened or closed, fans or air conditioning turned on or off, and thermostats adjusted.

Offering plates and candles which have been unthought-of until it is too late can be a source of embarrassment. Whether the offering plates should be at the front or the rear of the sanctuary before the offering is received, the ushers should make sure that all of these are indeed in that appointed place. If lighted candles are to be in evidence during the service and choir boys or acolytes are not assigned to ignite and snuff them, the ushers should make sure that the candles are burning before the worshipers arrive and put out after the worshipers have departed. Occasionally a candle burns too quickly, drops wax, or falls from its holder, requiring the prompt, yet as inconspicuous as possible, attention of the nearest usher. Candlelight services call for constant and special alertness on the part of all ushers, particularly if children are taking part.

Bulletins, and any other material which is to be placed in the hands of the worshiper, should be in the possession of the head usher well before the beginning of the service. These, with any special instructions about their distribution, should be given to every usher before the first worshiper appears.

WAITING

The usher has arrived and reported for duty some twenty or thirty minutes before the stated time of the service. He has taken part in making the sanctuary ready. He has had time to help with any necessary errands. He has received full instructions regarding every detail of the service which is soon to begin. There has been time for him to meet with the other ushers for a brief prayer to prepare themselves for the effective performance of their duties in the service. Now he waits. He is at his appointed station and, far from displaying a bored air, he is ready to greet the first worshiper to approach. At the conclusion of the service, the usher again waits, for he can often be of further help to the departing guests by answering questions, running short errands, and fulfilling any other need which may arise.

THE FINAL SURVEY

After the benediction and closing moments, some members of the congregation usually leave promptly, while others gather in groups to talk. But the ushers are not finished — there is more work to do. It was at this point in one church that a man was discovered sound asleep in one of the pews, unaware for a suspiciously obvious reason that the service had come to an end. It was clear that it was the duty of an usher to sit beside him, shake him into consciousness, and tell him that the service was over and it was time to go, but that he was welcome to come to church whenever services were being held.

Aside from the unusual duty, it is the work of the usher to go through his assigned area to recover articles that have been left behind, pick up debris, recover bulletins from between the pages of the hymnbooks and Bibles as well as from the seats, and help to collect communion glasses if there has been a communion service. As nearly as possible, the room should be put in order for the next service. Unless the church is small, no sexton can do it all.

6. THE USHER'S CHURCH

To a STATISTICIAN averages may be significant, but there is no average church. There are all kinds of churches, with varying qualities. Churches may be described as from very small to very large, poor to rich, coldly aloof to very friendly, haphazardly organized to over-efficient, simple to highly ritualistic, and in any number of other kinds of extremes and in-betweens. As it is impossible to find any two people, even identical twins, who are alike in every respect, it is unreasonable to presume that any two churches are alike.

The differences among churches have a bearing upon the work of the usher. Consider, for example, the many differences between a church of one hundred members and a church of a thousand members. It would appear on the surface that the first would need only approximately one-tenth as many ushers as the second. However, many other factors might present themselves, such as the size and architecture of the building, the location of the aisle or aisles, and the number and locations of the entrances. And it may be more difficult for the smaller church to enlist two ushers than for the larger church to enlist twenty or thirty of them.

In light of these differences it is apparent that methods may vary according to conditions but the principles of ushering are the same under any circumstances. The usher in a small church may perform many tasks and greet most of the worshipers as his familiar neighbors whom he sees every day, while his counterparts in the large church are deployed to areas of the sanctuary and to a few specific duties. In the small church, the usher will face a greater proportion of people who are regular and dependable and who neither need nor want too much personal attention from the usher. However, regardless of the methods, the principle of introducing the guest to the presence of God in a friendly and restful manner is the same in any situation.

RELATIONSHIPS

In one way or another, the work of the usher is related to the interests and responsibilities of several individuals and groups in the church. Whether he is extending a welcome, discovering the name of a visitor, or receiving the offering, some other person, committee, or board has a stake in the matter. Thus, in his tasks, the usher is often in partnership with the pastor, the sexton, the deacons, and the trustees.

It has been said that the summary of the work of the Christian church is the making of Christians and the making of better Christians. Although this summary makes no comment upon any specific pastor's methods, it is sufficient to offer a broad insight into his dreams and motives. The ushers' and the pastor's interests overlap in the proceedings of the church service. What, then, does the pastor wish for his church's services? Among the answers to this query, it would be expected that the pastor would desire that strangers come to the sanctuary, that everyone be seated satisfactorily, that pews, temperature, ventilation, and lighting be comfortable, and that each person be so impressed as to desire to return. Thus, almost everything the usher does affects the ministry of the pastor. It is highly appropriate, therefore, that the ushers carefully consider every suggestion made by the pastor. Whenever there is a meeting of the ushers, the pastor should be invited to be present. He should be free to assume an active part in the discussions, and should make whatever suggestions he believes to be fitting.

The sexton, under the mandate of the trustees, is the caretaker of all church property all of the time. Before, during, and after each church service the ushers and the sexton inevitably meet each other in the performance of their duties. Occasionally this encounter generates friction and hurt feelings, but it need not do so if each one recognizes that the other is seeking to make the best possible church, regardless of the position he holds.

Problems concerning the room, its readiness, its contents, and its cleanliness are those which are within the mutual concern of the ushers and the sexton. An illustration is seen in the control of temperature. The sexton is at work on the days before the church service is held. At some time, he starts or steps up the heating system, regulates the thermostat, and constantly checks the thermometer until the end of the service when heat is no longer required. The ushers are on hand for only a fraction of this time, but they are more strategically situated to take note of any effect upon the congregation of sudden temperature changes. Ushers can make minor changes in the room itself to provide continued comfort or make further slight adjustments of the thermostat. But here is where the overlapping of duties with those of the sexton ends: Except in an emergency they do not go to the furnace and attempt to modify its performance, for this is solely the duty of the sexton. Good sense on the part of both the ushers and the sexton will bring about cheerful and helpful cooperation in every circumstance where their paths cross.

The relationships of the ushers with the boards of deacons and trustees are a little more remote because, with the exception of the deacons at communion services, these boards are usually not functioning actively during the church services. Nevertheless, these two bodies maintain a constant watch over any procedures which fall within their responsibility, and they may have suggestions to offer from time to time.

OTHER MEETINGS

Valuable service in meetings other than the stated church services can be rendered by the ushers. One or two of them might be assigned to the church school session where their help in directing strangers to various classrooms would be gratefully received. Church business meetings and banquets frequently present problems and opportunities for help. Those who arrive should be offered a friendly greeting, directed to the cloak room or rack, and ushered to a seat where the meeting is to take place.

Special guests should be received and treated as gladly and hospitably as though they were arriving in a private home. Their wraps should be taken and cared for and they should be offered the use of rest rooms. Well before the program begins they should be introduced to the pastor or moderator, or should be led to their appointed seat of honor on the rostrum or at the head table.

When the guest is a speaker, the usher should ascertain what supplies he may need for his presentation. Whatever these may be — a special table, chalkboard, chalk, pencils, visual aid equipment, the room darkened at certain times — the usher should produce promptly and unobtrusively. If the guest brings equipment, the usher has the opportunity of helping him to unload it before the meeting, then load it again after the meeting.

The usher should remember that the guest remains a guest throughout the meeting and should not be abandoned at its close to fight his way out or to wait a turn at the cloak room. His departure should be accompanied by the same warm, friendly attention as his arrival.

THE WHOLE TASK

We have used many brush strokes to picture the ideal usher. He prays, thinks, functions, and worships. We should now try to forget the miscellaneous dabs of the brush and see the picture as a whole. Whether man or woman, the effective usher is Christian, cultured, sensitive, calm, adequate, pleasing, well-groomed, courteous, kind, understanding, effective, and growing. He sees his job as big but not overpowering. He is always aware that his proper functioning can help people to come expectantly into the presence of the Lord, become renewed in the sanctuary, and depart with a sense of Christian mission in the world.

7. RECRUITING

CHURCH USHERS ARE TO BE FOUND IN THE CHURCH. They may be men, women, or young people. The decision that an usher must be of one sex or the other, or from a certain age group, or a member of the church is merely the preference of the church. Some churches have ushers of mature years and some use only young men. Furthermore, even though this book has been written in masculine terms, there is no reason why ushering should not be done by women. Many churches employ people from more than one age group or sex as ushers. No particular kind of person is necessarily right or wrong for the responsibility.

A deacon, trustee, or member of the board of Christian education often becomes a superb usher. He has been chosen to serve because he has qualities which command respect. He is peculiarly qualified to be a skilled specialist in helping people. The careful screening received by a person when he is elected to any of these boards is proof that the people want him to be their representative in selected work in the church. This is not to say, however, that ushers may not be recruited from among many who have not been elected to office but who, nevertheless, are noticeably fitted to be ushers.

There are those who believe that most of the ushers should be recruited from among those who already have a responsibility for the inner workings of the church, and, on the other hand, there are others who believe in challenging as many individuals as possible to the task. As always, there are two main concerns to be considered, namely, getting the work done well, and inspiring individuals to do it well. To emphasize the first of these objectives means that only experienced, concerned persons should be enlisted. To emphasize the second purpose means that inexperienced persons will be recruited in the hope that, despite some errors and clumsiness at first, they will grow in proficiency.

When it has been determined that ushers are needed, the church moderator, the chairman of the ushers, and the pastor may draw up a list of prospects. They, or one of them, may then visit each individual listed to discuss the scope and opportunities of ushering and invite the individual to share in the work. Or the matter may be handled by the nominating committee. Another technique of recruiting is to invite all interested persons to attend a meeting at which the whole work of the usher will be outlined. In lieu of a visit, a recruitment letter might be sent to prospects (see Appendix for sample).

APPENDIX

THROUGHOUT THIS BOOK, references have been made to letters and charts. Samples of such helps are in the following pages. Moreover, this appendix contains two important items: (1) a check list for ushers and (2) suggestions for growth.

RECRUITMENT LETTER

Dear_____:

The psalmist speaks of his pleasure in being "Door-keeper in the House of the Lord."

Would you have an interest in being on the ushering staff of _____? We do not request a decision by return mail, but we ask you to consider this invitation seriously at a meeting on _____ at _____.

At that time we shall go over some high spots in the manual for church ushers, called *The Work of the Usher*. After you have seen the outline and scope of the ushering task, you will be in a better position to make a decision.

May we know whether you can come to the meeting on _____?

Sincerely yours,

Head Usher and/or Pastor

(This letter, as well as the following one, may be altered to suit any special conditions in the local church.)

ASSIGNMENT LETTER

Dear_____:

As Chairman of the Ushering Committee of _____
_____, I am sending you a schedule
of Sunday appointments for ushers during _____
_____. Please plan to be ready to usher at
10:40 each Sunday you are scheduled. If I do not hear
from you, I shall know that this schedule is suitable for
you.

In the event you cannot usher on the Sunday or Sundays scheduled, let me know and I shall try to rearrange
the schedule.

If the schedule is satisfactory on the whole, but a Sunday comes when you cannot usher, please do the following:

A. Call another usher and make arrangements to exchange with him. (See back of ushering schedule for names, addresses and telephone numbers of all regular and auxiliary ushers.)

B. Call me or the acting Head Usher to give notice of the change.

My personal thanks to you for the service you are rendering your church and your Lord.

Sincerely,

Head Usher

ASSIGNMENT CHART

	APRIL	MAY	JUNE
FIRST SUNDAY	Floyd Blair, Head Ira Barnett Timothy Fox Henry Nelson Gene Ames	Oscar Metz, Head Gene Ames Floyd Blair Fred Brinton Oliver James	Carlos Rio, Head Emil Rudolf Gus Hadley Boris Penza Donald Frey
SECOND SUNDAY	Floyd Blair, Head Fred Brinton Oliver James Carlos Rio Bruce Flint	Oscar Metz, Head Carlos Rio Bruce Flint Emil Rudolf Gus Hadley	Carlos Rio, Head Oscar Metz Milton Arcot Ira Barnett Timothy Fox
THIRD SUNDAY	Floyd Blair, Head Oscar Metz Emil Rudolf Gus Hadley Boris Penza	Oscar Metz, Head Boris Penza Donald Frey Milton Arcot Ira Barnett	Carlos Rio, Head Henry Nelson Gene Ames Floyd Blair Fred Brinton
FOURTH SUNDAY	Floyd Blair, Head Milton Arcot Ira Barnett Timothy Fox Henry Nelson	Oscar Metz, Head Timothy Fox Henry Nelson Gene Ames Floyd Blair	Carlos Rio, Head Oliver James Bruce Flint Emil Rudolf Gus Hadley
FIFTH SUNDAY		Oscar Metz, Head Fred Brinton Oliver James Carlos Rio Bruce Flint	

Names, addresses, and telephone numbers of all ushers are on the back of this sheet.

CHECK LIST FOR USHERS

A check list is useful in guarding against overlooking any details. Every airplane pilot knows that disasters are prevented by the simple checking of even the most elusive detail. Thoroughly, prosaically, sincerely, and without boredom the pilot recognizes that every check point is an assurance of a successful flight, remembering that the lives of his passengers, his crew, and himself may be lost if only one little item is forgotten or taken for granted. The usher, too, can profit from such a list.

The usher's best friend might refrain from mentioning some little detail which is offending or irritating. The following list, therefore, serves as a reminder. The usher should be mature enough to know how to care for each item.

Item	*Suggested Standard*
	PERSONAL
☐ Suit (dress)	Dark, clean, pressed
☐ Tie (accessories)	Subdued color, neatly tied
☐ Shoes	Black or dark. Polished
☐ Shirt	Clean, neatly laundered
☐ Hair	Clean, combed, well trimmed
☐ Nails	Clean, manicured

☐ Teeth	Clean. Nothing in mouth, including gum or cough drop
☐ Hearing	Keen. Hearing aid permissible
☐ Voice	Clear and friendly
☐ Flower, badge, or nameplate	In place
☐ On time	Twenty or thirty minutes before stated time of the service

MANNER

☐ Friendly	Subdued, not jovial or rollicking
☐ Helpful	Think from the guest's viewpoint
☐ Respectful	Know that all — young, old, rich, poor — are worthy of respect
☐ Prayerful	God's leading and blessing are needed
☐ Understanding	Alert to physical handicaps and the needs of children
☐ Thoughtful	Each person is a child of God. Remember name and seating preference
☐ Inconspicuous	Meet every need unostentatiously

SANCTUARY

☐ Clean	Sexton's job, but usher may help
☐ Pew racks	Everything in place. Pencils sharp
☐ Light	Adequate, not blinding. Protect pews from direct sunlight
☐ Air	Temperature and ventilation closely watched
☐ Offering plates	In proper place

☐ Candles, other ap-   Lighted. All accounted for
   purtenances
☐ Church bulletins   Ready for distribution
☐ Ready for next
   service

FUNCTIONS

☐ Greeting   Most people appreciate welcome
☐ Seating   Only at indicated times. Give guest
                 a bulletin as he enters pew
☐ Offering   In unison and according to master
                 plan
☐ Tending   Awareness of all possible emergencies
                 and knowledge of how to meet them
☐ Worshiping   The usher is a participant in the wor-
                 ship
☐ Waiting   Before and after the service
☐ Promoting   Encouraging quiet and a spirit of wor-
                 ship throughout the building
☐ Cooperating   Working in harmony with other ush-
                 ers to complete a total task

SUGGESTIONS FOR GROWTH

1. What is the gracious and helpful thing to do?
2. What is meaningful greeting?
3. How can I do better teamwork with the other ushers?
4. How can I help to produce an atmosphere of worship in the church service?
5. What can I do to stimulate congregational participation?
6. How would Jesus usher if he were in my church?
7. How can I help to recruit and train new ushers?
8. How is ushering done in other churches?
9. How completely do I carry out the pastor's aspirations?
10. What are some peculiar or individual needs in my church?

AN USHER'S PRAYER

Be with me, Lord, as I greet in thy name.
May thy spirit of wisdom and grace be upon me
As I gratefully serve in thy house of prayer.
                                        Amen.

INDEX